ALL TIME HUMANITIES SHORT POEM

P. SENTHIL M.SUGANYA
S.S.INAKSHI

ISBN 979-888521605-0

The Books the magic in poetry and a glossary gives names to those devices. It unpacks them. I believe its purpose is to deepen the reader's initiation into the mysteries. Here, then, is a repertoire of poetic secrets, a vocabulary, some of it ancient, which proposes a greater pleasure in the text, deeper levels of enchantment.

Contents

Contents

Contents

Foreword

Published By: Sushisen Publications

Address:

Dr P.Senthil S/O N.Periyasamy

1/197 Varagubady (PO),

Near Govt Middle School,

Alathur (T.K), Perambalur (D.T), Tamil Nadu, India

Toll Free (India) – 9965969652,9043636168

Pages: 88

Price: Rs. 145/-

Preface

The Books the magic in poetry and a glossary gives names to those devices. It unpacks them. I believe its purpose is to deepen the reader's initiation into the mysteries. Here, then, is a repertoire of poetic secrets, a vocabulary, some of it ancient, which proposes a greater pleasure in the text, deeper levels of enchantment. In the fast changing and competitive world of today, the ability to communicate effectively is perceived for the students of all disciplines. However, it becomes more informative and imperative for professionals who are dealing with technical forms of communication English as a medium of spoken communication, e.g. e-mail, facebook, twitter, Whatsapp have emerged and the form of language skills are used in these channels is having profound influence on student's language skills, especially when creating documents.

We are indebted to N.Periyasamy(late) and P.Chinnaponnu for his unstinted support to the faculty. We express our appreciation to P.Nallusamy wife of N.Lakshmi child N.Nagulan, N.Varnisha varagupadi or varagubady for inspiring and guiding us from time to time. Providing illustrations and samples respectively and also moral support.

We are grateful to our students whose aspirations served as a great inducing for writing this book. We also wish to thank to publisher for their careful and fast processing of the book.

Acknowledgements

This Book is made possible through the help and support from everyone, including: My wife M.suganya and Daughter S.S.Inakshi. We are indebted to N.Periyasamy (late) and P.Sinnaponnu for his unstinted support to the my parent. We express our appreciation to P.Nallusamy wife of N.Lakshmi child N.Nagulan, N.Varnisha varagupadi or varagubady for inspiring and guiding us from time to time. Providing illustrations and samples respectively and also moral support.

Prologue

Which is true
Seeing in person is a lie
Asking with the mouth is also a lie
Listening to the ear is a lie
The truth is what you see on WhatsApp

1. Beauty girl

Standing in front of you for a long time
Reed hair on the head of the cluster
Wide forehead brightly colored
The eyebrow hairs sang a new kind of poem
Both shoulders are like mature bamboo
The nose and eyes are neatly carved
The end of the face is the foundation for the birth of beauty
Cheeks black and green
Hands disconnect the desire to be able to thicken
Inside the moment I saw you
A wave of the vibration of the abyss beat in the heart
I felt like I was hitting a rock
Shame on me for stopping me
I saw you unbound all over
I was burned when I saw what you saw
Blood flowed from the soles of the feet to the scalp
The green blood also jumped
Turn off the copper-colored lord and join me
I will die even if it is delayed for a few seconds
Didn't leave after seeing no worries until seen

2. Natural

1.Ecstasy

Neighbors embraced together in love

Compromise without quarreling with the fight

Kanda Diniyanar Dignified Life Art

The ecstasy that appears to be about the ancient custom

2.Passed

Waterless white clouds

Waiting for the rain to fall on unpaved roads

As if you could live in a world without me!

The landless sky is waiting to glow in the pitch darkness

As if you could smile in a world without me!

Malignant seeds are waiting to germinate in dry land

As you can believe in a world without me!

Introducing the tweaks, you tricked me into running away and hiding in this world!

Allow only my writing in your world of ignorant ignorance ...

Let them be quiet without wavering!

More about this source text

3. Lover

1.Did not stop

In the green meadow,
A beautiful bird,
Injured in the leg,
Seeing him lying on the ground,
I terminal to handle,
That is automatic
To imprint her leg
Unable to try,
Fell and then got up,
Still not stopped,
Until the morning ...

2.You are the lover in the heart

Crescent moon in blue sky
Full moon in blue eye
You ate in the evening
The hair is airborne
You came with a smile
In the spring
Sprinkle turmeric in the evening
Near the heart of love!

4. I found love

Male: "I saw the beauty!
I wished!
I saw the poem!
I fell in love!
“I saw the beauty!
I wished!
1. Female: I saw the image,
I'm asleep
killed,
I found the relationship
You gave my life,
Male: Is this love?
Is the dream real?
Is stealing a pleasure?
Are you at my disposal
Woman: I saw the sight!
I feel sorry for you
I saw the season!
Affectionate
See you soon!
I feel sorry for you

5. Human

1.People

Male: I found sweetness,
I enjoy
With me,
Reluctantly,
I mitigate
boldly came,
Woman: Is desire real?
Is love a condition?
Are you willing to give?
Is it a playful day?

2.Daily morning

The red rose smiled at the lotus
Morning view of the eyes impressed
Scatter pearls over coral petals
You came as a poet and fell in love in the morning too!

6. My favorable

Although anxious
Although blindfolded
Although I am dry .... !!!
Although walking down the street
Even if the lamp is turned off
I still look at the sky .... !!!
Even if it comes in half
Even if the skirt falls off
Although I am a sinner .... !!!
Even if the twilight goes on
Even if the universe stands
Although I think with desire .... !!!

7. You are the heart of love

Heart you are in me
Why do you love her
In the sky if she could see
You are flying
Alone if she gets angry
You are suffering
You gave me the pain of love
You're gone
Her heart is within me
You kept it hidden
She loves me
You are addicted
Live me with her smile
You keep
Love touched me
Are going
She is looking for me

8. Love

1.Count me

Although over noise is surrounded ..
Only my intention
Surrounding you ...
What is the reason
Not yet known ...
To know the reason ..
If you want to explore ...
Will love diminish in fear ....
My life and soul ..
Melts to see you ..

2.Have to write poetry for eye-popping love

Have to write poetry for eye-catching love
The eyebrows should be painted for beauty
Browse in the sky and the moon in white
You are the only competition for the water lily!

3.Love language in the blink of an eye

Love language in the blink of an eye
Girl River Magazine Smile
The celestial faces
Poetry in the beauty of the western sky
Wait for you dear!

4.Love

Even without the moon
The nights pass .. but,
Without your memories
My nights have never passed ...

5.**My God**

Goddess
Love Tao
Rebuke father
Teaching Asano
The fountain of my excitement
The abode of my emotion
Jump air show
Mathura music
The enchanting nature
Lord of life
Who are you
To me

6.Awake

Come and speak disparagingly
He gives the night
Proverb hundred by word of mouth
Will give a gift
You will not tell the way
Grew up thinking
Awake mouth dawns
Eyes to see!

7.Way

Direction four will delight you

You will also enjoy the place where you stand

Yellow coated face

Marik is kind of fat

The desire to build is going to steal everything

It is invisible to the naked eye

Do you long to touch?

May thirst to continue

8.Sky

Sprouted in the sky

White Moon I .. !!!

Without crying me out

You are the ruling father .. !!!

I love the burning about the feet mind

You are the burning light in me all thinking .. !!!

Color to the eye

This is the love that will continue to fade into the sun for a long time .. !!!

9.comfort

I do not understand what love is

Desperate for anything

The mind itself opens the mind a little

Dwell there; on him '

Love desire

That is to cross the ocean of samsara

Para is the love of comfort

10.Love is sweet

The one that fell in my view
The one who entered my mental sky
Snatch me up
Gone
In day and night thinking
Existing
Who thought she was
I was eager to say love
Time without looking at her
Wandered in search
I finally saw her
I asked for consent
Angry face
The moment when the smile blossomed

11. Excessive love

On the pond lotus
With excessive love
Fish-like eyes
Loop with
Pray to Brahman for blessings,
Near the lotus
Spend a lifetime
By excessive desire
Did you appear as a fish?

9. Life

1.Good - bad

Good news
Bad news
Birth or death
Nothing is permanent
Everything is unstable
Got it once
Enjoy life

2.Pain - way

Why only me so much pain
Counting as - to recover from it
Think of it that way

3.It rained

In her chest
Leaking moisture
As it rained
I climbed the mountain ... !!

4.My life

Like the melody to the song, like the grammar to the poem
What came into my life
This is the meaning of life
What is not vain praise
This is the truth of the matter

10. Enjoy life

1.Do not worry!

Do not be swayed by the pursuit of misery!
Do not lean when encountering happiness!
Do not be discouraged when victory comes!
Look at the flowers .....
Because it is the sanctuary of God
Because it is the grave of man
Does not change from her character
Bloom like flowers
Enjoy the fun you get !!

2.Mortgage

Night time sleep
Leave the pawn to the cell phone
We are unable to recover ... !!!

3.Heartily

Near to tighten
Although not - within me
Heart is forever

11. I like the moon

To see your beauty
Near you
I want to be cloudy.
Flower!
To see your beauty
Near you
I like to be leafy.
Night!
To see your beauty
Near you
I want to be a star.
Dear!
To see your beauty
Near you
I want to be imaya.
Beautiful!
To see your beauty
Near you
I want to be a lover.

12. Mahabharatham

1.Duryodhana - Sakuni

Have to beat five, Uncle!
He must destroy the clan
Tell me a way to it.
No need to fight, nephew!
I will spread the web of maneuver for him
I'll let the dice fall, he said
I will gift you the Goddess!
Sakuni also crowed
Kauravar dug a hole for the clan.

2.Duryodhana - Thirudharashtra

My lord, hear my father.
Let's invite five to gamble.
We will send the invitation.
We will wait for his arrival.
We will defeat the needle.
We will look at his caste.
The king's edict is required.
Everything else is uncle work.
We have made a decision
No change in the end anymore.
Elder, teacher, certifier
Not to ask anyone.

The king's order is required.

The denial was unacceptable.

3.Thirudharashtra

Want to dance to the beat?

Why do the maneuver?

Why disturb the peace?

Why seek destruction?

Why should we commit this sin against the Pandavas?

The child must be protected before disaster strikes.

Descendants must recover from the clutches of sinful Sakuni.

A thousand questions and desires arose in my mind.

Yet child affection prevented the blind there.

This,

It is time for the nomads to leave Astinapur.

Scholar, it is time for adults to fall for superiority.

It is time for the world to curse Sakuni.

4.Thirudharashtra - Viduran

The blind man gave the order, viduran

That the mission should go

Could not deny, widower,

There is no strength in the mind.

Unable to resist, Sakuni,

Could not break the poison of.

What is education and gaining wisdom?

Seeking out a crowd of dogs

Has been. Viduran, Andy raised him physically

The Pandava carried the sin towards the land.

5.Daruman agrement

The message from Vidur was not surprising
Nothing has changed in Astinapur
Maneuvering has not changed, and enmity has not changed
Sakuni has not changed, his conspiracy has not changed
Daruman knew the maneuver that was in the call
The work of destiny is to give it
Felt
To refuse the invitation is to insult the father,
Let's play a little dice game and come back
Let's see and come back Let's look at the word hatred
We accepted the invitation and we will come to Astinapur.
The five of us will greet you! See you soon in Astinapur.

6.Ground

The five arrived at Astinapur
Those who come as kings will become slaves
Go to the royal court and present gifts
Worship all of the scales adults
After the squirrel has eaten and rested slightly
Sakuni, the Saniyan, started the conspiracy
"Let's play dice! Let's have fun!
The competition is all about fun! "
Daruman slightly rejected Sakuni's invitation,
"Dice game is a game that promotes enmity
We must try to eliminate enmity itself
Betting takes place within the enemy
Why should this gamble within the natives?

There are many good ways to have fun.

The dice game is not for us to play!

7.Sakuni

Are you scared? I thought you were the king!

I thought he was a hero but I was surprised

Enormous wealth, man, arrow, army

Can you lose in front of this poor uncle?

Do not be afraid, let's roll the dice!

Daruma hesitated and bowed his head in front of the plot.

Destruction embraced everyone well

8.Daruman concept

You came to play dice uncle but what do you bet?

Aren't you the king?

I will dance with my immense wealth.

What will you do? You just relied on speech.

9.Sakuni

Don't worry, I'm off the field too.

Is my son-in-law's wealth my wealth?

If I put one I will put nine in front of it

Let's fight! Let's go in search of luck!

10.Rule

Vithura justice is all wasted

No one listened to what Patton said.

Dronaer did not open his lips thinking of the word he had eaten.

It is customary for the mother to respect the father

Not in Astinapur

Man has lost his temper in the church of everything
Became demons, lost the recipient,
The learned art is forgotten, the weed is lost.
The game of ghosts will continue. Great evil will result here
The dice will roll here and many tricks will occur

11.Game

What's up with the game?
Oops!
Daruman's famed cock floor tapping.
The concept of the king symbolizes peace within.
Man, arrow, army, all pochu.
Understand the truth of the game.
Sakuni's plan is known to all.
Daruman has lost his house.
Madayan has decided to keep the country and dance.
Sakuni rolled the dice and Sakuni won again.
Daruman, who had lost the weeds, stopped to kill the anxiety.
Sakuni continued, "Daruma, why are you reluctant.?
Brother, there are four of you, you have the right over him,
What more hesitation, bet him
Not over yet game, give it a try and you too "
Daruman agreed and risked his brother
Defeated one by one, Daruman died four times
Thampi lost himself after the four left
There is no longer any property to pledge.
There is no point in continuing the game.
Sakuni is not leaving, the border has not yet been reached.

"Panchali is still there, will you! Can you risk her?"
She has the power to rescue five.
He will search for your luck with her "
This is the last arrow thrown by Sakuni
This is the foundation of the Indian War.
She is the light of the Pandava eye, the daughter-in-law of this Bharat
Younger than Kannan, equal to Parasakthi
To the Honorable, she is the essence of this poem
"I risked our goddess, roll the dice"
Said Daruman
The dice rolled and the sinner Sakuni won again.
Kannan rushed to Astinapur with the sari in his hand.
They lost royal life and became slaves,
The caste line is full of drink today.
The dignitaries bowed their heads in the congregation.
There is no one in the corrupt church to listen to
A lot of deaf people joined the church today with the blind.
The pride of Astinapur became the sunset
The gamble that Sakuni made destroyed everyone.
Drag and drop! Slave, wife of five.
She is no longer a queen, she is still a slave. "
Duryodhana ordered and smiled ugly.
Accepting the order, the policeman rushed to the spot
He described all the tragedies that had befallen them
The king's order must be obeyed
The mother was angry like a battered serpent

"I am the queen. Tell me, not Dasi."
The slave has no right to risk others.
I do not accept any order.
This is my order, you can go. "
Time to bring destruction and see beauty
It's time to dump her and move on
Arpan was agitated when he heard his mother's answer
"Brother Tussadana, drag her!"
The beauty of slaves, drag her! "
The brother gave the order,
The wicked villain dared to sin.
There is no word to say the cruelty done by the wicked
The woman's mind was not known
Her suffering was unknown
No screams or roars were heard
Arpan pulled about his mother's hair
The gift received by the Pandavas was thrown in the middle of the assembly.
She cried and cried for justice
Kannan called her brother
She cried and reported her condition
"Pavier this Pandava lost me on the needle.
The Bedouin crowd despised me as Dasi.
All who made love became slaves.
The demon is trying to shape my grief.
I want to protect my dignity, I want to get rid of pollution. "
She called Om Namo Narayana.

She forgot herself. She participated in that Mayan.
Called and received grace, with grace
Clothing also grew
Tussauds shrugged
Kauravar's blood froze in fear.
The purity of Panchali is manifold.
Panchali slowly opened her mouth
She thanked Parthasarathy
She touched the edge of anger and shouted loudly.
"This is not a council of men, it is a congregation of Ali.
A crowd of people who can't protect a woman's dignity.
Meeting of the Goons of the Blind Government.
This is the crowd that sold the Kula Vadhu gooey.
I am no longer Bhadrakali but Panchali
I am the death knell for the Kauravar clan
Agni's daughter I have no boundaries anymore
No more trust in the male class
I am no longer Pattini for Pandava Five.
This is the beginning of destruction, and there is no more peace.
The hair could not, and she did not lose her temper.
Dushtan Duryodhana had to split his thigh
The sinful villain must break his shoulder
Sinners want to wet my hair in the groin.
The clan of the blind must perish.
Those who have lost their minds should go to Mandu. "
Panchali swore and left the congregation alone.

13. Travel

1.Life travel

What is self-awareness?
What do you get if you know yourself?
If anything,
The one who knows himself is everywhere ..
Self-knowledge for the world?
For fame and desire?
Get rid of desire
Do you want to know yourself?
Many sages, elders, ascetics
It was the game I tried.
I need to realize why
Why only me this question ..
Friends, all round
Sesame laughed,
The next thief is ..
When Ramana entered into himself and knew,
After sitting on Annamalaiya,
When death is felt alive,
The experience of knowing oneself?
He is his experience
Others can not speak completely,
Search, language, as needed

Grace will set and deliver.
I thought confused guru
Remembering in the middle of the eyebrows
I called the Guru and blessed him
I forgot the Guru on the wave of memories
Traveling ...

2.Listen

“If the mind listens and the body does
It is a relationship,
If the body does asking for knowledge
That’s it.

3.True memories

Even if living realities appear before our eyes
Although lifeless memories do not appear
Eventually pressed deeper
There are only real memories ....

4.Mother

On the ground
Slightly irritated with irritability
Iconic vines for small ruffles
The mother who gave herself

14. Poet

1.Poet queen

She is devastated
Not at all
She is a beautiful woman
She is a thousand
Of Nayantara
Of two thousand Meena
The beauty is the same
Received in the form
To the moon
There is only one difference
If you travel the world it is the moon
Traveling around the globe can be a daunting task
Like her tooth
If seen
University
The government will not build one
Everyone's hair is just touching the head
Only her hair is touching the floor
She must have been born to a rabbit and a peacock
In the heavens
Twenty years
The angels are all looking for Urvasi

Not knowing that she lives in our town
She is not the creation of her mother
She is not a creation of Brahman but a creation of Goddess
247 characters in Tamil
Only five characters in it sound so good
The letters that come with her name

2.Life for yourself

Life for yourself
At the evening meeting
Lost to you
Searching my heart
Reach out and hold your hand
Continuing my
The journey of life
Even when you fall into your trap
I bloom with unconditional love
Even if you talk less
You give less love
In loneliness without you
Your memories
Is coming around in you
Surrendered my heart

15. The Eyes

Where did you come from
Where did you go
Nothing is known
I do not understand anything
Hey darling!
You are beyond the sky
Came from.
You are in the depths of the abyss
Came from.
Like honey in a flower
You came into me.
The breeze touched
The storm is gone!
The bow broke
Come by the indicator!
Pluck the stars
Come on in, Danta!
Dear dear
where did you go?
Into your eyes
I'm missing!

16. Heart

1.My heart

The form of a loving child
Creepy on the lap, lullaby sung form
Art painting that blossomed within itself
The joy of seeing in the form of a child
Day is a naughty divine mind!
With a smile on the blushing face
Forgot himself! When I do not see you
The pleasure that dawns at dawn
Epic child full of house
You slept soundly on your lap
Mane with countless drops of love!
On the day when your eyes were engraved on me!
Wherever you go you remember me
She got up and walked under the Buddha Bodhi tree
A flower-like shower of penance
Moon-like face shining beauty
At the doorstep of any guest chemist
Colorful bird waiting! You!
You are full of mind! Our feast!
Girl who runs tirelessly like a clock!
The umbilical cord that flows through the mind is fragrant
I heard your voice..in those minutes!

Forget me -your idiot
Memories of the days lost in the voice are still there today
Your soft voice has never been heard before
Loving words do not perish in memory
One star in your name is Swati!
Can not forget! The heart bank you surf
As the income I have saved
I'm still imprisoned today!
To this day liberation is not available
I'm a lifer!
Eyes remember your figure
Keep copying.
My sweetheart to you forever
I long to live by the image!
Where did you go you did not find in the soil
Waiting for revenue! I'm awake!

2.Sweetheart

No longer this one - as
According to the movement
You directed me !!

17. Memory

Came and went
I do not know
In your memory .... !!
Injuries and passions are one
Attack together
In your memory .... !!
Intoxicated with love
Injury blindfold
In your memory .... !!
To pose faces
I fall into denial
In your memory .... !!
Hidden hidden love
Enchanted with seconds
In your memory .... !!
Even though regrets hit me
I'm still alive
In your memory .... !!

18. In the view of the night

Which whenever you see
The little heart never beat
Love has never been bitten by the eyes whenever seen
The tip of the ear lobes
Mustaches are not brushed
Once a minute in distant moments
Never called and inquired
Although a few second conversations are enough
It never lasts longer than hours
Rural yellow fever
After confirming the ownership,
Nadi did not hold on to the silky gold pet
The desire to choose clothes is never given
In the mornings when the monster leaves
Fill the empty stomach
Never fed
Nostalgic for outings
Never buried in the photo
The living atoms come together
Even after the birth of new life
Not once did he dare to think of the word love

The listener never introduced the name with the place
Called birthday, wedding
Greetings or gifts
The joy of sharing was never shocking
No matter how many times we stare
Never thought of breaking up
I was able to write love in thousands of poems ...
So far nothing has been written for you
Damn you do not want to give up on the opponent even if everything burns down
Let's just keep stacking like this
Lots of Itiyathi Sangams !!!
Bury during the day and keep the chin at night
Steal sleep
The surfer is obsessive
Still in these poems
I keep it hidden
Stinky old food
Tingling in the green veins
This is something you only felt !.
Not only is it unwilling to market but it is also tempting
The mind of the conspirator!
Yet behold my days are old
After the nights are over
You are your Yatsani who fights
Throughout the period
Everything I write is not for you, it is for me, my God !!!

19. Memory

1.I am in the grip of memory

The lonely moon in the blue sky
Chasing clouds
To chase away memories
With a tired heart
I'm a sea urchin!
Unannounced storm
Your angers that come meaningless
Staggering to dissolve
My heart!
The tear of the medium
With love
you always
All over the wall of the heart
love give time
On
In the tidal sea
We played foot wet
Dissolve together
Sports footprints
You left the coast ...
Today
To continue you

Dissolve as matoma
Like a throbbing wave
In my beating heart ....

Stitched love
Water through the eye
Peek ...
Of chasing you
I'm completely in the grip!

2.Her vision

The sharpness of the said wall was also blunted
She blinked
The sharpness of the wall breaks the heart of Eid
Her vision is in the heart
Stitch grows adding love
What a vision she said me

20. Mercy

"Will Kantan have mercy?
Will the situation change?
Will Kumaran grace come?
Works less?

Did you ride a peacock?
Forgot the beauty of the hand wall?
Biofertilizer,
Mind flexible,
Keep your eyes wet
Tears flow
Searching for myself, (Kandan)

What is the story without Arumugam?
What is the God of Comfort?
Come longing
Come on Anbil
Think of you

21. Room

1.My Room

In the sparrow crowd
I'm excited - my
Inside the small heart room .... !!
When alone
Do not hesitate to accept - me
Inside your love room .... !!
In a state of turmoil
Save and drag - yours
In the love room .... !!
While in the vicinity
You won by crying - yours
Inside the room called Warmth .... !!

2.Life Room

If the individual sells alcohol
It is counterfeit liquor false income.
But if the government sells
Alcohol with power through Tasmag,
It is revenue to the government.
If he fights not to have both of these
He is insane These are the positions of all the state.
If that changes, this government is the light of the Lord.

22. Power

1.Money

Money is the lifeblood
By all means.
Money owns
Will attach.
Surround yourself with friends
Distancing enemies.
Seeking influence;
Fame is raining.
Positions will be sought.
Many comforts are available
Power comes from money.
The benefits to the city are many
can do,.
Fertile for relationships
Can guide. .
Happiness in the lives of the poor
The light can be crowded.
And money without arrogance
And money that does not show luxury
Will bring in more money

.

You to the world of money
Identifying ..
Of life if there is money
Ideals will be fulfilled ..
Money belonging to goodness
Is the paradise of the world.
Money educates;
Good for offspring
Gives a comfortable life.
In life with money
Successes will come.
Born into life
It's achievable.
Money is its source
We will add money;
We will work hard and save money.
Money gives everything

2.Mathura in the smiley face

Soft flower Rose bundle
It's time for you to come
My poem praises you

3.Her vision

By her eyelid my
She opened my inner eye

23. Flag flower

To see your smile
The day blooms in the evening
In the scent of hyacinth
Self-boiling head
The forgotten flower
See the flag flower daily
To the Creator and to Hades
I will go and fight
May you be the Buddha Malarai on the flag
Mannavanum dying in your lap mayankukiranati die
Green rice toothpick
Ambush yourself with ripe mane
Let the tertiary come to you like a flag
Flag flower Flag flower on me
Anger is something for you
You are missing the point
The Buddhist flag Malarai in my mind

24. In the view of children with mouth caps

This is the gate of the windy M school
Waiter,Thank you for the evening
We want to warm up this school student,
You are not a mouthpiece,
you are a babysitter. Yes!
Standing on one leg,
With patience,
Found many in pride,
The charity that did the water until yesterday,
Because it has aged today
On normalcy.
Asking for a little language,
Walk with your heart erect!
Coast working for them!
They enjoyed the hike!
What more to say?
We look forward to more debit,
The help you received is beyond words.
You waited for school all day,
You also saw this as your home,
You said the truth works,

Not just for you,
The reputation of the school
Added,
Rest for you from tomorrow!
That's all there is to the study,
The body needs it
A little rest,
But for your hard work
Fatigue will never go away.
You are going to get the answer today,
Idayura found peace,
With uninterrupted pleasure,
To be happy.
The evening of tears
That it will dry out in the heat,
Make the evening of events,
make the memories its scent, shoot, accept!
May you have all goodness
And prosperity and live in peace, Lord
We will answer your prayers. "

25. Nature Love

1.I LOVE YOU

I said out loud
The sound of any voice
In your ears
Surely Sounds great ... !!!
But ... something ...
still you Silently Are you ... !!!
Of your silence
Without understanding the meaning I suffer ... !!

2.Nature

Thorn Surround hope
The pink flower of the s fill
In the creeping breeze
In the loot garden
Flower rose
She is coming to pluck with a thin finger
Will the two snatches me together?

3.The coconut

Radiation that opens into the south ventricle
Coconut juice ivory sweet
You are the honeymooners who lean on the coconut
What's next?

26. Home

Wife people, furniture,
Utensils
Bundle knots,
Pet dog, cat herd
Getting in the taxi
While moving house
To look back and sign,
Helplessly in the yard
Standing mango
The dried fruit and leaf are like shade
Giving for free
Take care of yourself and nurture me
Stuck alone
It's like asking how the mind came to be!
That's it
The answer is go and come
Refuse to go
Do you know how to report ..

27. True love

There is love in your eyes
Why do you look at me
Anger is coming
Keep the love deep
Are
Why not tie it on me
You are hiding
The other one scolding me
Location
Let me come straight to you
Location
My name is tattooed on your hand
What is the reason for the stabbing
I sincerely apologize
To you
Speak a word you say to me
My life is with you

28. World Father

I seek God daily and repent
The God of weight will come down to me
Soil we are yours
Human resouce
You saved us by thinking
God bless you
Of going to heaven
I have no intention - I
The festivities are not great
Lord repent and me
Will accompany you

29. One Day

1.That one day - for her

Dear hands
And fibrous lids
What went unnoticed
To appease my heart a little more

As full of my love everywhere
Imprisoned for feeling
Deaf to some
Before your eyes
To me standing
You froze yourself a little
As my love
I was a little upset
Wholeheartedly
A thousand runs
Countless questions
You will be heartbroken if you ask
If your eye leaks
My love is in turmoil
So I refused to listen
All unacceptable
You agreed

By your tears
I accepted for my love
I wiped away the tears though
Wholeheartedly
I gave the shoulder
Half-hearted
One minute to forget everything
You just stood by my girlfriend
As shown by the love shown
Let the troubled heart stop
To flood the sidewalk
A little off
Stopped me
I was stuck in a trance
My love though
This is the last text
The final moment with you
Pulsed a little to fill
Solidifying the mind
Magic smile
Withered face
New spring to be born
The words spoken are numerous
In the weeping weeping eyes
To be born a bliss
I worked so hard
She forgot to laugh

Forgetting himself
She smiled slightly
It does not dissolve at all
I kept it that way
That scene is complete
Countless conversations
Forget the place and happen
Words that fail to say
Reach for some ear
All the words spoken
Though mind boggling as to where
Counting her completion
Passed, for her comfort
Except for my love
There is no other denial
Cross the clock number
To be like this is to beat the mind
Ranamakki mind love
Finally a trip
Only two songs
Memories are heartbreaking
All that was kept in the shake reservoir
If tears drain
I comforted her for that too
Finally in that moment
I tried to see her smile

In a state of turmoil
I have never hurt my love
That's what love is to me
Although parted with pain
My love is so sweet
Even if love goes away
The scenes do not deviate
That one day is not for her
It was for my love

2.Her beautiful poem

Each of your elements is a symbol of beauty
If fiction by words is beauty poetry
Composed by the Lord with beautiful elements
You are the love poem of nature
Let my thoughts lie dormant in you
I forgot myself in your mind
Aren't you a beautiful poet?

3.Depression!

In a body without feelings
looking for the figure
you are crazy................

30. Taste

1.Loneliness

The cock is heated
Boiled
Then cool
The filter sucks
Rainwater and lust
Loneliness
Favorite to taste

2.Fulfilled

It is an expression of happiness
This sweet kiss,
To the honey of the lotus
With equal taste !!!

31. My life is for you

1.Imagination of love

Do not imagine
Did not see you in the dream
Didn't go looking
The angel will come as a lover
Do not know
God bless you
No word
She had me in mind
Loves
The desire to live with me for many generations
She is lying
She is as rich as the poor
Did not see
Hunger for her for affection
No.
My life is for you

2.Girlfriend

Girlfriend in friend ....
Can stay awake for several days ... but
Could not be without longing even one day ....
You are the one who melts in your memory! ....

32. Life memory

I know
Here's to soaking me
Rain coming down the threshold
Definitely for him
Of earlier days
Weck hand
May be rewarding!
In the sense of feeling and not feeling
Except for the rain
Behind the doors
Hides
By his views
Woven my love!
This was after a rainy night
In my face
A name for sure
May sound
It did not even inform him
That would be the nickname I gave him
Please do not tell him if the name falls on your ears
He has a family there !!

33. An unwritten poem

Whenever desires arise
Let's see - in it
I admire you all ....
Whenever coming face to face
Thrilled - that
I magically disappear in a trance ....
Whenever with
Dissolve - in it
I speak to you ....
Whenever I was asleep
I see - they are
I want to be without art ......
Whenever thinking
Glad - that
I live thinking of happiness ......
But,
No matter how much you write
Whenever writing
You are an impossible poet
Within me
You are an unwritable poem ......

34. Mirror

The girl will not paint you
Even for the typography I write about
Named as female
Wrote many poems and sent them to you
Put
You do not understand my thoughts
Put
Love has awakened
Growing up without looking at time
Is going on
Waiting for her is new
Sounds like a thrill
Mind you to see my pair of pigeons
Beats
The place to look is everything she is
The face itself is visible

35. Same

Looking forward to something
This day and night
Do not fight
Are moving
Why only we continue
We are still fighting ..
Extreme advice everything
The smoke dissipated
In a couple of months of not seeing
Single chocolate in hand
You bring and stretch
With a smile
As sweet news ...
Crushing to the bottom
I lost something
"Why are you a model"
I left without asking !!

36. Inakshi

Married to sister
Three years later
Beautiful baby girl
She was born.
They to the child
Named 'Inakshi'
"Beautiful Hindi name
None of the world's Tamils
To their children
Unnamed name "
Were proud
Sister and uncle.
And the next child
If the girl is born a baby
Its name
What would be
Not beyond my imagination

37. Feminism

In the community,
Because the girl
If you want the offer,
Do not ask for equal rights ...
With men
Equal rights
If desired,
For being female
Do not ask for offer ...
Have the right
Have the privilege
If so,
Only men
For equal rights
Have to fight ...
Girl ...
Rights ,
Offer ...
Anything
Take ...
But,
Let the men live too ...

38. Passion

Darkness to the moon of
Top passion!
Staining the wave
Top passion!
The oasis to the breeze of
Top passion!
Rain to the soil of
Top lust
Beauty to the woman
Top passion!
Money to man of
Top passion!
Innovation for youth
Top passion!
Wisdom of old age
Top passion!

Food for lives of
Top passion!
Each one of
Top passion!
A priceless love is a priceless love ..... !!!

39. Lamp

The eyes did not sleep
You did not come in a dream
Remember yourself wherever you look
Wave
Love flower shower in the chest
Scans me
Snowfall in the month of Karthika
Love I still have her
Not holding
The right leg is still my
She did not keep at home
Her colossus osai n
Did not listen
She is still in my eyes
Did not fall
When she lights up
Didn't seem to be coming

40. Beauty (Fire)

Caste for aesthetics
No religion!
The killer flower
Shame on her!
the hair when the window is opened of
The smell is on the nose!
To the music of her colossus
Do not let the stones on the road sing!
colour to own
Do not go like a yellow river!
One of the star in the sky
Hold your nose!
Like the Amazon River
The curve is intertwined!
I thought it was blurry
New honey in mind!
The addition does not count
Have a great day!
Tradition abounds
Will you nurture my heritage!
Dear nearby Will it last for life !!!
To ignite the forest of love
You are a (fire) !!!

41. Lips

In the rhythm of light
The condensed sound
Ambush cat keep your feet down
Descending in the night well
With the stars there
In the rosary of darkness
The combination of the moon
Slides in still water
Throwing and laughing well neem
With dense branches
Fleeing the leaves
The window sill of the room
Whispers Shredded Light and sound
Scatter the clothes
Dissolve life Of playing markers Hysteria
In the scorched forest Of hens Krr Krr noise
Chen water will sprout
On the lips traces of teeth
Aside hide
Taste the clamshell
To him and her
A thousand lips!

42. The pulse of love

I blinked
Yourself
I stand watching
Your silence
When to dissolve ... !!
My ears are eager too
Stay tuned
Of your voice
To hear the sweetness ... !!
My heart was beating too
Stay tuned
Your heartbeat
With all my heart
To connect ... !!
These are all me
Will be put on you
The pulse of love
Understand that ... !!
My physical substance is spirit
Everything is for you
Realize that ... !!

43. Towards love

Your vision of love is me
Flows towards
Without asking permission from me
Entering inside my heart
Is over
Showing off its beautiful figure
Is over
Giving respect to love
Is over
Starting to show its work
Is over
Unloving lives in this world
Saying no one
Is over
It is God who created love
As has been known
As love is to be enjoyed
Sent to me
Both hearts change location
Gone all

44. Carry

Revenge, for sin
The one who walks in fear
That coward
Complaining men
Take the picture and play
The one who killed the snake
Great hero
Will celebrate
Almighty made
Strange though
Respect for justice and honesty
The walker is the hero,
Bad behavior
Without justice, honesty
Spoil until next
The profit seeker is the coward
Just live alone
Humans who understand many of the evils
Those who think harm
Merciless evildoers,
The poor by hand
By the grace of waiting-- yourself
In the heart of the living

45. Flap of a flower

Why did you roll your eyes
My heart is overflowing!
When I came to you
And your past
And my opposite period
Forgotten
You are on the side
The one who leaves the picture
I love the beauty of sight
I am with Padik
The feminist I love
Written to another
Love letter
With his own hands
Will deliver
Postman model
On the one on the side
The one who leaves the picture
I love the beauty of sight
I am singing
Your memories of me
Kicking and playing
I became a pawn

I get to sing
Applause with enthusiasm
You are one in the crowd
You are sitting
Your memories of me
Kick and play

46. Life Distance

1.Second marriage

“No more
Even for a minute
Can not live ...
Just look at your face
Do not want ..
Get lost ... ",
That parted
My first wife.
‘For me
You are everything ’,
Those who said,
Going to be someone
In the lives of some
Becomes inevitable.
A
On Good Morning,
Our divorce
In court
Determined.
That’s all
Not easy,
After the permanent partition,

Loneliness.
Eleven months
After desert isolation,
Again
An angel
On the path of my life
She interrupted.
To me
Second marriage
Because,
At her house
Did not accept us.
As a way
My second
After marriage,
For me,
First night
Or
Second night.
One thing
I will say,
But, do this
If you are studying,
Me
Don't plan ... OK ...
'To my second wife
This is the second night. '

For that
Why brother,
That's the plan
Do not think ...
The reason is the next para.
"Hi..hi ...
Divorced users
It was my first wife
My second marriage
I got married ... "

2. The love of distance

With sea distance search
Find yourself
Neo remote found in search
Before the moon can go what needs to be done
Distant moon
Like a child eager to see
My mind was searching for you
Lost is once again a sea voyage

47. Who

Where did you come from
Your figure is unknown
The one who does not fall into the trap of your love
No.
Love is for you girlfriend
No restrictions
You are an indescribable poet
nobody is here
Something that you heart to live
Not yet in this world
You do not need an introduction
Telling anyone you're coming
No. Is to connect two hearts
It is your duty
The daughter of love keeps shaking
The chariot of my life
She spruce up
After thinking with the partner
You are the only one who makes me happy

48. Daughter-Pain

I ran away with dreams
I spread my wings to fly
I had wounds in my heart without lying,
You wanted to reach me in the form of a man
Me when the Guru thinks
You crouched down
Femininity is forgotten as a gender,
Something lingered between my chest
Can't remember why it has a heart in it,
This condition is why my skin is frozen
The shape is the same, only the face changes
Affection in your mother, in me
Lust also seemed to be something
As long as I was in the oven, nothing happened
That's why we were in the cage
If you are trying to suppress your desire
Is this female freedom?
The fault is mine, yours wandering mind
We are victims of temptation
If my breast attracts you
We were ready to dissect it
My lady gave you lust
We are ready to distort my femininity

Beware of the angel of justice
We are in the sanctuary of the Lord
When the paper is crushed, you
The criminals will also be the tent of men
You are blindly trusting them there
If the country and the rivers have a female name
Does that mean respecting the woman
We flooded the motherland and exploited the rivers and lakes
Did we get the name of a country where women do not deserve to live?
This is our pride
The three-year-old child was the first to live and finish
Regardless of the woman until old age
Barbie just in case
With so many questions like this
I am the queen

49. Two Match

My friend said,
"Friend ..
For love
Can give life too.. "
I'm terribly angry,
'For your love
It is fair that you give life.
Taking my life
In what way is justice ...?. '
This
Like the second paragraph,
In my life too
Two matches ....
In the match,
Whatever wins,
The impact is only on me..
First match:
Corona,
For my wife's cooking ...
Who first me
To die.
Second match:
For my signature

To my caption.
What could be worse ...
In both matches
Both
again again
Winning ...!
it's me
To you
I have already said,
Of this poem
The third para ... '

50. All One

Dear colleague
Not without an address
This removed the facial line
The letter is for you
Not written exclusively
Whether early on
Let me tell you
Like writing
Not easy
Your name
To read ..
However why in the diaries
In daily tweaks
Your name anywhere
Not tapped
Secret vaults
Even the password
The smell of that name
I do not remember consuming ...
Your counterfeit
Flavors
In memory chips
Search

Bored
The sea dried up
In a day
Suddenly introverted
Single hair

With a rotating tongue
Only once
Now your name
I want to pronounce
Woody taste
The curse of the buds
Unlimited heavy iron
Refuses to move
Nervous tongue ...
This letter that was leaked
In reading
Don't get bogged down in lines
Scold (nju) vayo?
So on the day you demand
Pull the fuss
Fear of coming
It hurt in the end
Surrender
And clever words
To you as always!

Like figs
The address you sent
Overcome theories
The chronic that was stolen before joining me
Pollen of your SMS bouquet
Precede the heart
Even forgetting like me
In any of these instincts
Do not let the heart scatter ...
In distorted images
To get stuck
Undoubtedly
A (U) may be laughing !!!
Just like writing with the mind now
Not easy
To read your name ..!
Dear Saga This is an unaddressed letter
Not for you
To deny yourself the right to praise
I have no reasons!

Author Details

Dr P.SENTHIL

MA,M.Sc(Maths),M.Sc(IT),BEd(SPL),MPhil,PhD.

State:Tamilnadu

Country: India

Education: PhD or Doctorate

Affiliation: Kurinji College of Arts and Science

Domain of Research: Technology Trends,Intelligent Systems,Artificial Intelligence,Artificial Neural Networks,Autonomous Robots,Big Data,Data Mining

Biography: P.Senthil was born Varagubady(village) in Tamilnadu in India in 9 May 1987.He received his B.Sc., degree in Information Technology from Bharayhiyar University for coimbatore, Tamilnadu.He was received the M.Sc Information Technology and M.Phil degrees in Computer Science from Kurinji College Arts and Science,Trichy ,Tamilnadu in 2010, and 2014, respectively. In 2012, He joined in the Department of Computer Science,Kurinji College of Arts and Science in Trichy,Tamilnadu as a Lecturer and now He is working as Associate professor in the department of MCA, KCAS College of Arts and Science,Trichy Tamilnadu from June 2014 onwards. He is doing his research in Image mining & Digital Image processing at Bharathidasan University, Tamilnadu in India. He is the examination board member of various Colleges and Universities and He guided more than 6 MPhil Research scholars for various universities.

M.Suganya MA,BEd,MPhil

Education: MPhil

Affiliation: National Arts and Science College

Domain of Research: Indian poet and Novel Writer.

Biography: M.suganya was born Trichy in Tamilnadu in India in 13 july 1993.She received her BA English, degree in Kurinji College of Arts and Science , Tamilnadu.She was received the MA English Barathidasan University and M.Phil degrees in English from National Arts and Science College ,Trichy ,Tamilnadu in 2010, and 2014, respectively.

9 798885 216050

Printed by Libri Plureos GmbH in Hamburg,
Germany